TO:

FROM:

HOW TO CREATE
CRAZY SUCCESS
FAST

88 DAYS
TO ANY
GOAL

DR. ROLLAN ROBERTS

IGNITEREADS
spark impact in just one hour

simple **truths**
▶ Small books. BIG IMPACT.

Internal images © page v, Reinhard Krull/EyeEm/Getty Images; page viii, mihailomilovanovic/Getty Images; page xii, Chris Ryan/Getty Images; page 9, Hero Images/Getty Images; page 20, 33, 58, Thomas Barwick/Getty Images; page 28, Kittiyut Phornphibul/EyeEm/Getty Images; page 34, Donald Iain Smith/Getty Images; page 39, Michael Blann/Getty Images; page 44, Peathegee Inc/Getty Images; page 50, David Madison/Getty Images; page 74, d3sign/Getty Images; page 88, MarioGut/Getty Images

Internal images on pages 14, 19, 22, 25, 42, 47, 54, 56, 60, 63, 64, 67, 69, 70, 72, 76, 78, 80, 84, 92, and 94 have been provided by Pexels and Pixabay; these images are licensed under CC0 Creative Commons and have been released by the author for public use.

Internal images on pages 2, 5, and 6 have been provided by the author.

Published by Simple Truths, an imprint of Sourcebooks.
P.O. Box 4410, Naperville, Illinois 60567-4410
(630) 961-3900
sourcebooks.com

Printed and bound in China.
OGP 10 9 8 7 6 5 4 3 2 1

This book is dedicated to my daily source of strength, support, favor, and provision—my Lord and Savior Jesus Christ.

Everything I do I also dedicate to my parents, who have provided unwavering love and support when I was a hotshot CEO and when I was sleeping in my car for months hoping to stay warm and find food. Other friends and family deserted or distanced themselves from me and couldn't handle the deep valleys and tremendous pain that forged the massive success. I saw the breaking and brokenness as building, pruning, and refining. My parents never stopped believing the calling and anointing on my life and knew that the deeper the brokenness, the bigger the blessing. I love you, Mom and Dad!

MASSIVE SUCCESS can be achieved, momentum gained, and groundwork laid with eighty-eight days of all-out focus. **SUCCESS LIKES SPEED**!

TABLE OF CONTENTS

INTRODUCTION

ONE OF THE MOST unspoken, critical keys to success is the 88-Day Promise. It's the all-in, full-out, all-day-every-day, early-in-the-morning-until-late-at-night, full-court press commitment for approximately twelve weeks to achieve massive results. Seven days a week. No days off—just the pure, relentless pursuit of a single worthwhile dream or goal. With one day of planning and the last day wrapping up how far you have gone and where you are going next: eighty-eight days to any goal.

Success does not warp itself to our time deadlines. It may take seventy-seven days, eighty-eight days, or ninety-nine days for the 88-Day Promise to take root in your life and produce results. The 88-Day Promise is the principle behind *88 Days to Any Goal*. You can do it in eighty-eight days, but the process is broken down into twelve equal weeks and three post-process recovery weeks.

Everyone I know who has been successful in anything—business, politics, their career, religious or social causes—at one point or another did an eighty-eight-day run or series of eighty-eight-day runs to get to where they are and accomplish what they have.

How many books have you seen on this principle? While it is the single biggest factor to achieving massive results, very few people ever talk about this aspect of success. In the seventy-five-plus years of the personal and human development industry, there currently isn't a single book on this topic. Maybe that's because it's not sexy. It doesn't make success sound easy and appealing.

But my audience understands that anything but the truth is fluff, and they aren't interested in fluff. There are enough "gurus" that will make you feel all warm and fuzzy about just being you. My focus is on building champions, winners, people who do not lose in life or business, and it will not happen without the 88-Day Promise. *88 Days to Any Goal* walks you, step-by-step, through all twelve weeks and what you need to do the three weeks following the 88-Day Promise to not lose the results. Spend the next thirty-four minutes discovering how an eighty-eight-day commitment to a single objective will profoundly change your life, family, and future. That's the Promise.

SUCCESS LIKES SPEED

IT HAD NEVER BEEN done before in Montana state history. By all researchable accounts, it had never happened in 225-plus years of American political history for that matter!

Oh, there have been some close electoral races. There have been some David-versus-Goliath battles where David wins or comes close to winning.

But in every single one of those races, the winners had time and/or money. There was planning,

positioning, strategy, and sometimes even years of setting the stage for the upset.

A no-name who's not originally from the state, with no political backing, no war chest, no years of campaigning and building relationships, and no political capital going against one of the most powerful, influential, well-connected, well-funded, decades-in-the-making legislators in the state and coming sixty-four votes away from winning the state senate seat—that had never been done before. And I did it in ninety days.

You can spend years, even decades, struggling and grinding along, hoping to get to where you want to be (e.g., losing weight, making money, building a business, recording a hit movie or song, or writing a bestseller) and never get there. Or you can do an intense, eighty-eight-day, all-out blitz that can do more to get you to where you want to be than years of consistent effort and struggle. And that's the 88-Day Promise.

The military takes physically and mentally unprepared young recruits and turns them into stalwart personnel in the program called boot camp.

Many fitness companies have challenges where they want you to follow their program for ninety days to lose weight and get in shape.

Many people have gone from sloppy and overweight to well-groomed and lean by committing to the 88-Day Promise.

Entrepreneurs have gone from anonymity to rock star–status with the 88-Day Promise. They've gone from two or three people in their business to having one thousand people at an event, and they did it with the 88-Day Promise. They've gone from making a couple hundred dollars per month to making above $10 million over the next seven to ten years—all because they did one 88-Day Promise.

Artists, musicians, and performers have gone from deep, dark obscurity to national sensations because of the 88-Day Promise.

What you have been searching and working for—that elusive dream—may only be accomplished with the 88-Day Promise.

The bigger the dream, the more impossible the goal, the more certain it will require the 88-Day Promise. It will be the most exhilarating, exhausting, and inspiring eighty-eight days of your life.

I did the 88-Day Promise in 1998 and built a real estate empire when I was nineteen years old. Everything I accomplished during those next couple of years was a direct result of my 88-Day Promise.

During that same period of time, I did the 88-Day Promise and built an exciting direct sales business that resulted in me personally sponsoring seventy-two people my first year.

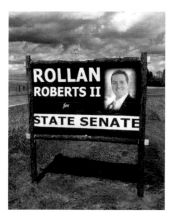

In 2004, I did the 88-Day Promise at a multibillion-dollar, publicly held company and became a senior executive responsible for nearly fifteen hundred employees.

In 2006, I did the 88-Day Promise to regain control of my weight and lost seventy-five pounds over the next eighteen months.

In 2010, I did the 88-Day Promise at a direct sales company to create their first growth month in fifteen years and became the president of the company.

And that's where the story of my most profound 88-Day Promise begins...my race for state senator.

THE CAMPAIGN

I STILL DON'T KNOW what I was thinking. *It will be fun! It will be a great experience. Why won't anyone stand up for what they believe in? I can make a difference!*

It was February of 2012. I had just left my position as president of the direct sales company and started a nutraceutical company.

Two weeks later, I heard a sitting legislator lamenting over the voting record of a state senator, arguably the most powerful in the state, and how no one was willing to challenge his seat in the upcoming election.

The sitting senator was an incumbent, fourth-generation Montanan, second in command—president pro tempore—in the senate, and by all accounts would preside as the president of the senate in the 2013 legislative session.

He had never had a primary opponent, despite numerous attempts over the years to find someone willing. No one would run against him because he was a bully. Whoever challenged him would pay—win or lose.

There was a contingent of people who were outraged by his deceit and voting record. He told them one thing and then voted another. He said one thing to their face while campaigning and then did the opposite when it came time to hit the red or green button.

There were a few issues that were especially important to me. There were millions of dollars at stake, based on whatever budget passed that would have major implications for years to come. His voting

record and the district's viewpoints did not line up. I felt that my principles better represented the majority of our district than his voting record did.

The election was on Tuesday, June 6, 2012. Absentee ballots went out thirty days prior. I basically had around eighty-eight days to win this election.

People betrayed me. There were scandals, bribes, secret polls, and personal mudslinging. My odds were slim to none going in, and several times throughout the campaign, slim walked out the door!

On the last day to file for the seat, a third entrant jumped into the race fifteen minutes before the deadline. This completely ruined any chance I had at winning, because according to conventional wisdom, we would split the vote and the incumbent would be reelected. All hope was lost…whatever little there was initially. The impossible became complete insanity. My campaign was over before it began.

I decided that I could win even with insurmountable odds and even though all the experts said the math and data just didn't add up. They were right. They really were. The math didn't support any path to victory.

But as one of my mentors would say, **"If the dream is big enough, the facts don't count!"**

I had one thing that all the data in the world couldn't compute. Belief. I had belief, and with a little bit of faith and belief, miracles can happen. I wouldn't have started the race if I knew belief was all I had, but once I had started, I realized that was all I needed.

I had close to eighty-eight days to help thousands of people get to know me and what I was about. They needed to feel like they had known me for years. They needed to be comfortable with me. They needed to be able to talk to me, call me, and meet me.

I created the strategy to win the same way I would write a business plan for a company to win. Granted, I normally have more than eighty-eight days before a win/loss score!

I created the ground-game strategy—volunteers

for calling, door knocking, holding signs, and getting campaign materials out.

I created a media strategy—put out anything the opposition could possibly use first and be totally transparent with the public about my flaws and short-comings. It minimizes the sizzle if I tell people my imperfections up front. Someone comes to them and says, "Did you hear that Rollan...?" And they respond, "Uh, yeah, it's on his website," or "He mentioned that in a speech." Takes the air right out of gossip.

I created a position on how I would interact with my opponent. I would not say negative things about him or his family. I would strictly and vehemently express my viewpoints on his voting record and how they did not adequately reflect the views of the district.

I would spend all my time talking about what I believed in, not what my opponent did or did not do. I wanted people to vote for me—not against him. Of course, I'd take those votes too, but my mentality was to win the hearts and minds of the people!

I created an online and offline marketing strategy—web ads, SEO, AdWords, print ads, a media kit, mailings, phone calls, surveys, speeches, and interviews.

I consulted with national advisers who had devoted their lives to state and national politics. I sought counsel regularly, because I knew that this was a David-versus-Goliath battle. I was the underdog. No one gave me a chance.

They didn't know me. They knew my opponent, even if they didn't like him. It was the devil you know compared to the devil you don't. Neil Postman said, "People in distress will sometimes prefer a problem that is familiar to a solution that is not."

THE MAGIC OF 88

IN 2006 AND 2007, I lost seventy-five pounds as a result of following the 88-Day Promise. As an entrepreneur, I had an eighty-eight-day system where I would go into companies and create the infrastructure that would allow them to double their revenue in twelve to twenty-four months or do complete turnarounds. Regardless of industry or unique set of circumstances and resource constraints, it was in place at the conclusion of eighty-eight days.

Success is created through consistency over extended periods of time, but it starts with an 88-Day Promise. It's consistently doing the right things and having the right "life" system that makes it so.

Most successful business owners and entrepreneurs I know can trace their success back to the first eighty-eight-day spurt they had. Depending on the level of their success, they can probably share several more eighty-eight-day sprints they had as well. In every success story, there are key defining moments, decisions, and actions that were taken. If they weren't in the 88-Day Promise mindset, they would have made the wrong decision. Since they were, the rest is history.

The magic of eighty-eight is knowing that success isn't neat and clean. It's not eighty-eight days and poof, the magic unicorn appears. *88 Days to Any Goal* is the reminder and expectation that your 88-Day Promise is not calendar-driven but behavior-driven. Summer, fall, winter, and spring don't start and end right at the 88-Day mark, and neither will your journey.

Success is always messy. Success is always a grind. You will have to overcome fear, rejection, hurt, pain, and betrayal. Magic doesn't happen on day eighty-eight; it happens each day you give everything you have to a specific goal for eighty-eight straight days. The 88-Day Promise gives you the right mindset and expectation that focuses on the daily behaviors, the critical few, not the clock.

It takes close to eighty-eight days to implement systems in business, sports, and life that can take any company, team, or individual to the next level. It's how long it takes to see profound results from changes made in your personal life that can establish a lifetime of successful habits.

The new behaviors and actions you take during the eighty-eight days become habits. They actually reinvent your life and transform it, because your successful habits and decisions come naturally after eighty-eight days.

There has been much training on the four stages of competence:

 Unconscious Incompetence: A baby can't tie her shoes and doesn't know she can't tie her shoes.

 Conscious Incompetence: A child realizes she can't tie her shoes and gets frustrated when she tries.

 Conscious Competence: A child can tie her shoes if she concentrates on it and thinks about what she's doing.

 Unconscious Competence: A child can tie her shoes while she's texting, having a conversation, and surfing the web.

The 88-Day Promise takes the unconsciously incompetent and makes it unconsciously competent. That only takes eighty-eight days when you do an all-out blitz. It takes years with a "slow and steady wins the race" mentality, if it happens at all.

I was with a gym owner in Boca Raton recently who has built an incredible following based on his ninety-day body transformation challenges. As we were discussing the eighty-eight-day principle, there was a wall beside me full of before and after pictures of people who had made absolutely phenomenal transformations in a ninety-day period of time.

Permanent change can take place over eighty-eight days of doing the right thing.

Eighty-eight days of massive commitment and massive action with no reservation. Risking it all with everything on the line and everything to lose—time, money, reputation, assets, character—everything.

The 88-Day Promise is about being vulnerable. You might fail. In fact, you probably don't want to know your odds of winning. But those don't matter anyway, because they count all of the people who didn't fully commit with an 88-Day Promise.

One thing is for sure; you definitely won't get there without it. The 88-Day Promise is inevitable for people who win big.

THE CRITICAL FEW

WHEN YOU ONLY HAVE eighty-eight days, you learn the distinction between the trivial many and critical few very quickly. In any 88-Day Promise, there are usually only two or three things you absolutely must do to achieve success. There will be hundreds of good things (the trivial many) for you to do, but not at the expense of the critical few things that are of highest priority.

The key to success with the 88-Day Promise is

going all out doing the *right* things. The right things are the critical few.

My commitment to the cause and the campaign grew with each passing day. As articles came out—for and against me—they strengthened my resolve. I started writing bigger checks and investing more time campaigning. Within just a couple of weeks, I was completely consumed with the mission. And that's when my eighty-eight days really started. Your 88-Day Promise doesn't start until your bank account and calendar prove it.

I got better at saying who I was and what I stood for. I got better at listening to different political advisers give contradictory advice and then at making the final decision when they all knew more than me politically. I got better at knowing what to accept and reject. And I started to understand the cycle.

It gets real fast when you have people camped outside your door spying on you every day, creeping out your family. It gets real fast when people go

through your trash trying to dig up anything they can. It gets real fast when tens of thousands of dollars are spent on opposition research from top national firms—meaning "Let me pay you $100,000 to dig up every spec of dirt you can on this one person."

You think a due diligence background check for the high-level job you're getting is rough, how about I employ a company to do nothing but find every little flaw or perceived flaw ever! Not cool.

June 6, 2012, came, and I lost by 111 votes. On Wednesday, June 7, mysterious votes that were previously missing surfaced and showed I had actually lost by sixty-four votes.

That meant that if I had persuaded thirty-three more voters to vote for me instead of my opponent, I would have had enough votes to become the next state senator!

However, this wasn't the loss that it seemed. My opponent lost his heir-apparent position as president of the senate. I had successfully taken down the most powerful legislator in the state of Montana. In *David versus Goliath: Part 2*, he experienced a humiliating victory, and I had a victorious defeat.

Since then, my influence has significantly grown around the state, and numerous doors and opportunities surfaced as a result. In addition, it gave my constituents the chance to see how a leader handles defeat.

So what field of play do you think is too high for you? What level do you think you're not ready for yet? What level do you not feel worthy to be playing at?

That's where you need to be. That is how you know you are in the right place.

THE BREAKTHROUGH

THINK YOU MADE A mistake starting a business? Are you second-guessing your decision to get fit? Thinking you are not cut out for your new career? Are you reconsidering the 88-Day Promise you committed to?

Ten years from now, you're going to say one of two things: "I'm glad I did" or "I wish I had."

Win or lose, success or failure, I can say, "I'm glad I did. No regrets."

The honor is not in never making a mistake,

never losing, or never failing. The honor is in finding something worthwhile and fully committing to whatever you've chosen to pursue—win or lose. It's about the race, the run, the 88-Day Promise—the person you become in the process.

Just because I lost didn't make me a loser. It meant I lost. I, Rollan, was still a winner. That never changed. In fact, losing in that manner has supported me a whole lot more than winning would have. It let people get to know a side of me that for most people is their ugly side.

You may not get the exact results you want in twelve weeks. It's not about that entirely. It is more about what you create in those twelve weeks that carries you forward, something you never would have had had you not done the 88-Day Promise. And that's where the breakthrough comes from.

You will lose more weight after the eighty-eight days than you probably will during the eighty-eight days, but it's the eighty-eight days that create the habits and patterns that you carry from there on.

The systems and habits you discipline yourself to do during the 88-Day Promise will serve you more in the following months than they visibly will during the eighty-eight days.

You will make more money and have more success in the months and years that follow the 88-Day Promise, but it's the 88-Day Promise that makes that possible.

The energy and buzz that the 88-Day Promise creates are what will carry you in your endeavor for months and years ahead as long as you don't quit.

I don't run every day as hard as I did during the 88-Day Promise, but I have continued to be visible in my community, and I have supported and served community events since. It takes a lot less energy, effort, and finances to maintain the results of your 88-Day Promise than it does to go through it.

If you are in an 88-Day Promise where there's a scoreboard that's as clear as an election—yes or no, you made it or you didn't, you're in or you're out—win or lose with dignity. Win or lose with class. Win or lose as a gracious winner should.

Set the standard in victory or defeat. Losing will say more about you than winning, although I never lose even if I lose.

Ultimately, I have the mentality that a loss isn't a loss. A failure isn't a failure. I just lost more money than I made in that deal, or I didn't get enough votes, but I still had thousands of people who voted for me and supported me.

Legendary NFL coach Vince Lombardi reportedly said, **"In my entire career, I never lost a single game...I just ran out of time."**

And that's how winners think—even when they lose. Winning or losing does not define whether or not you are a winner or a loser.

You choose by your actions, responses, and habits whether you are a winner or loser. And if your actions, responses, and habits are reflective of a winner, then you will win more than you lose.

Winning is a habit. So is losing. Winners don't make a habit of losing.

For me, it wasn't just about winning; it was about running. It was about bringing everything I had and running the absolute best race I could. I wasn't competing or racing against anyone but my best.

And that is the essence of the 88-Day Promise.

6

WHY IT WORKS

THE SUCCESS PRINCIPLE BEHIND the 88-Day Promise is that you can accomplish far more than you think you can in eighty-eight days by committing to a single audacious goal focused on the critical few. You can accomplish more in eighty-eight days going all out than you can doing the same slow and steady activity for years.

Success likes speed.

If you are in sales and make one hundred phone calls

per day for eighty-eight days, your results are going to be significantly greater than the person who makes the same six thousand phone calls over the course of a year. You both would have spoken to the same number of people, but because you did it in eighty-eight days, you get results that the other person will never attain without doing the 88-Day Promise!

A real estate agent who prospects tenaciously and relentlessly for eighty-eight days lays the foundation for their entire career after a single 88-Day Promise. Realtors who never do this may call on more people, do more marketing, spend more money advertising, and still never get the results of the real estate agent who did the 88-Day Promise.

Direct sellers who do the 88-Day Promise usually make hundreds of thousands, if not millions, of dollars and never work at the same intensity level that they do during their first 88-Day Promise. Contrast that with people who have spent thousands of dollars on conferences, programs, books, and marketing tools who prospect the same number of people over the course of years but with miserable results and little financial rewards to show for their years of investment. There is no substitute for the 88-Day Promise.

Athletes who do the 88-Day Promise set themselves on an upward trajectory that lands them in the Olympics, professional sports, and state, national, and international championships. Those who do not never seem to have the same competitive edge. The difference—the advantage—is the 88-Day Promise.

Entrepreneurs who launch their business with the "slow and steady wins the race" mentality never get their business off the ground. Business owners, whether they've been in business ten days or ten years, who do the 88-Day Promise never look back.

The bottom line is that you will not get the same results doing the same amount of activity (calls, prospecting, marketing, selling, working out, or whatever it is for you) as the person who does the 88-Day Promise. They're going to do the same amount of work you do (or less), do it in eighty-eight days, and live handsomely off their results.

What you get by doing the right activity for eighty-eight days that you don't get by doing the same activity over an extended period of time is momentum, energy, and the magic of belief.

When you are in your 88-Day Promise, people know. They see it in your eyes. And those closest to you know the difference! They know when you're just trying something out, kicking the tires, or testing the waters. And they know when you're all in. They know when you're committed.

They can tell when you're so fired up and so inspired that you have to set alarms to remember to eat. They can tell when you don't hit the snooze button to get eight more minutes of sleep. They can tell when you're decisive about the hundred little decisions that come up during the day, because you are laser focused on your purpose.

And when prospects see the belief, excitement,

and fire in your eyes, they say yes to you. When potential business partners see your passion and commitment, they say yes to you. When a real estate agent has the eye of the tiger, their clients like and respect them, which gives them the confidence to say yes.

You will get less sleep than you're getting now. You won't be going on vacation, watching TV in the evenings, or golfing on Saturday. But you will be energized and inspired!

Eighty-eight days of intense focus on the right activity and the right behaviors can change your life forever. Eighty-eight days is enough to time to transform your life from rags to riches. Eighty-eight days is enough time to transform your body from carrying a few (or a lot!) of extra pounds to a trim, toned, never-felt-better body. Eighty-eight days is enough time to take you from a nobody to a somebody.

The 88-Day Promise is about doing the right things for eighty-eight straight days—day in, day out, with 100 percent focus, purpose, and passion.

And that's where the magic happens.

The 88-Day Promise doesn't begin when you start your business, sign up for something, join the gym, or register for a new program.

It begins when you make the decision to do the 88-Day Promise, as shown by your behavior, calendar, or bank account.

And when you decide to do an 88-Day Promise, you don't wait until tomorrow; you don't wait for Monday, next month, or January 1. You start now. The moment you actually make the decision.

The 88-Day Promise is not a logical decision; it is an emotional decision. You make it with your heart, not your head. That's why you can't wait; you must start now.

My eighty-eight days did not start when I filed for the campaign. It didn't start after creating the strategy. It started when my heart chose to be all in and my actions and commitment reflected that I was all in—campaigning day and night, then doing

organization and administration late nights and early mornings. Then rinse and repeat...for eighty-eight straight days. No complaining, just pure inspiration. It was inspiration based on a belief that this was possible. I wasn't looking for certainties; I was looking for possibilities. I could do this.

And so can you. Whatever your 88-Day Promise is, you can do it. In a world of can't, you can. In a world of doesn't, you do.

It was at the moment that I was all in that I strongly felt and knew that this was something I was called to do. I did not know at that time if I was called to win or just to run, but I knew that I was called to give that race absolutely everything I had. My calling was not to be a politician; it was to run the race. I was willing to do whatever it took to run a race that could guarantee the victory or allow me to hold my head high in defeat— because I was going to run a first-class race.

CRAVE THE INTENSITY

WHEN YOU ONLY HAVE eighty-eight days, you don't have time to play defense. You have to take massively proactive actions to even have a chance of winning. You have to look forward constantly. The second you start engaging in the trivial many, which is where the critics, media, and political hacks like to live, you lose.

It is a grind. It isn't sexy. And it's not something you'd wish on your worst enemy. The 88-Day Promise is absolutely grueling, but it's only eighty-eight days!

It's exhausting, demanding, and cumbersome in every possible way—physically, mentally, emotionally, and spiritually.

Running for the senate was a grind, to say the least. And it will be a grind for you. Whether you're in an eighty-eight-day program to lose weight and get fit, an eighty-eight-day race to grow or jump-start your business, or an eighty-eight-day preseason training getting ready for your professional sport, it's a grind. It's ugly. Some days, you're the windshield; other days, you're the bug. It's just the way it goes.

I never said it would be easy. I said it would be worth it!

The 88-Day Promise is about overcoming and defying the odds. It is about David taking on Goliath.

But Goliath has friends. Some of his friends live in your mind and tell you that you're inadequate. They put doubt in your mind that you're cut out for greatness. They suggest that you won't make it, that you

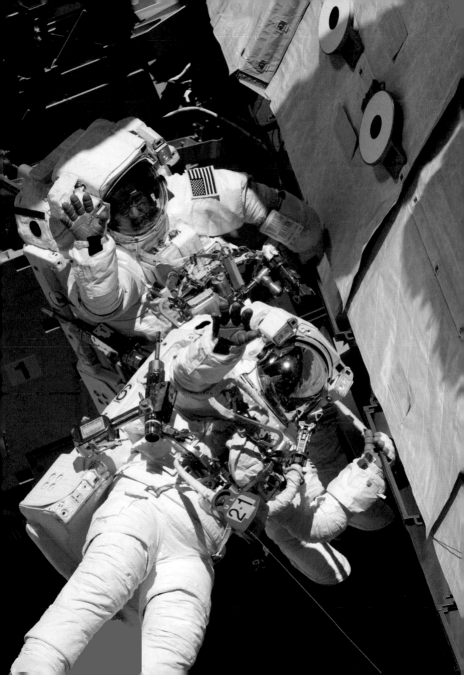

can't have the body you dream of, that you can't make the money or have the success you are fighting for.

The 88-Day Promise is really about you beating your internal or external Goliath.

You can win if you refuse to quit during the 88-Day Promise. Adversity causes some to break and others to break records. You just can't stop a person who won't quit.

The adversity gave me clarity. It fueled me. It inspired me. But I never got my "why" questions answered (i.e. Why is this happening to me? Why are they saying this about me?). They didn't need to be. And neither do yours.

Your emotions will be all over the board during your 88-Day Promise. You won't be super positive every single moment of every single day like you may be when you start. You won't always have a song in your heart, a smile on your face, and a spring in your step. You will get mad at times. You will get frustrated with your lack of results at some point. You will go from excited to discouraged in a nanosecond. You will likely have high highs and low lows and not even realize it because you are truly in your 88-Day Promise.

You'll have the chance to quit more than once. You may have someone, like I did, offer to pay you to quit! Your initial supporters, business partners, customers, or clients may tell you to quit because they didn't realize what an 88-Day Promise looks like and don't have what it takes to see it through.

But they don't know that champions are made when the stands are empty. Rock stars don't always perform to screaming audiences. It's the price you pay for success. Deals will come; offers will be made. Your resolve and commitment to your 88-Day Promise are all you'll have.

Winners are not afraid of losing—losers are.

8

OWN YOUR RESULTS

WHEN I TRAINED FOR my pilot's license, I was assigned a flight instructor who taught me on the ground, in the classroom, and in the air. When I got my scuba diving certification, I had an instructor who was with me every step of the way. I didn't know what I didn't know. When I started riding horses and motorcycles, I had trainers who started me with the basics and fundamentals. These were new endeavors, and I needed instructors who had devoted their lives to these particular skills to train me to be the best I could be.

When people start businesses, it's advisable they learn from people who have started businesses and been successful in doing so. People who have gone before them and have done what they are trying to do—that's how you speed up the learning process and minimize failure.

When people follow an eighty-eight-day fitness program or challenge, they have trainers, nutritionists, and experts guiding them on the journey.

Athletes have coaches, actors have acting coaches, golfers have swing coaches, and you need coaches, advisers, mentors, and experts to guide you if you're going to make the right decisions and swing the club and shoot the ball in a way that helps you win. It's all about taking the right actions during your 88-Day Promise! It's not enough to run hard and climb the ladder only to get to the top and realize it was leaning against the wrong building!

Surrounding yourself with the best you possibly can is critical. Coaches, mentors, and advisers are essential during your 88-Day Promise.

The vast range of emotions you will certainly experience, along with the fact that you should and will be in the trees and not be able to see the forest and big picture at times, are just a couple of reasons you need a team around you during the 88-Day Promise. They can instruct, and they can advise, but only you can make the final decision.

I remember one instance where I had three completely different recommendations—strong recommendations…win or lose recommendations—on how to handle a particular political situation. These three advisers were all extremely competent and some of the most sought-after political minds in the country. And they didn't agree. But a decision had to be made. And the buck stopped here.

You will have these defining moments too. You've got counselors, mentors, advisers, and a team of

supporters. They won't always agree. If you're in business, you will have a CEO saying one thing and investors saying another, while the company board or advisers strongly insist on something else. And you have to make the call, and it will not make everyone happy.

If you're on an eighty-eight-day fitness journey, you're going to have times when your friends will want you to celebrate with food or drink that do not contribute to your goals. And everyone you talk to will have a different path or approach to fitness and will advise

you differently on the specific details of your path. You have to make the final decision and go with it.

If you just embarked on a new entrepreneurial journey, and you've started or are in your 88-Day Promise, you'll have different leaders who prefer different methods of building the business, but ultimately, it's about you learning from each of their strengths and following a system that works leveraging your strengths and personality so that the system is authentically *you*. You must own it in your heart to be successful.

THE ANNUAL
PROMISE FORMULA

FOR GROWING COMPANIES, LAUNCHING products, building big businesses or incomes, staying in peak physical fitness, or achieving massive results, the 88-Day Promise is broken down into what each calendar year could look like. Success is rarely as simple as 1-2-3, and it rarely works out to be precisely seven days of this or thirty days of that. However, numbers like that allow certain behaviors to be tied to specific periods of time. The process is broken down into twelve equal weeks and three post-process recovery weeks.

THE ANNUAL 88-DAY PROMISE FORMULA LOOKS LIKE THIS:

✔ First Quarter—88-Day Promise

✔ Second Quarter—Post-88-Day Promise: Refresh, Regroup, Recharge

✔ Third Quarter—88-Day Promise

✔ Fourth Quarter—Post-88-Day Promise: Refresh, Regroup, Recharge

Plan, Do, Review, and Adjust with
All-Out Intensity and Focus.

88-Day Promise

WEEK ONE

✔ Identify a clear objective.

✔ Determine daily habits and schedule changes.

✔ Determine appropriate daily behaviors and activities.

✔ Identify the top two or three critical behaviors or activities that are required to achieve your objective.

✔ Implement changes immediately.

WEEK TWO

✓ Go a full week implementing your chosen behavioral and activity changes.

✓ Review what's working and what's not at the end of the week and adjust as needed.

✓ Develop a tangible or verbal action to do or say to yourself when you want to quit during the 88-Day Promise.

✓ Follow the "Plan, Do, Review, and Adjust" formula.

WEEK THREE

✔ Increase the intensity of daily activities.

✔ Identify schedule gaps and fill them with behaviors and activities that support your objective.

✔ Confirm your schedule indicates focus on the critical few, not the trivial many.

✔ Follow the "Plan, Do, Review, and Adjust" formula.

WEEKS FOUR TO TWELVE

✔ Be at full intensity, all-out behavior.

✔ Assess your attitude and have a provision to keep you engaged when you want to quit the 88-Day Promise.

✔ Commit to having no schedule gaps.

✔ Remove all distractions from your objective.

✔ Confirm your schedule indicates focus on the critical few, not the trivial many.

✔ Follow the "Plan, Do, Review, and Adjust" formula.

Follow this annual formula for one year, and your life will never be the same. Your finances will never be the same. Your career will never be the same. Your health and fitness will never be the same.

The Post-Promise Plan is very strategic to your success and, done right, will solidify your efforts and results during the 88-Day Promise and give you the stamina, desire, and energy you need to follow the annual 88-Day Promise formula.

Post-Promise Plan

So you just finished an exhausting 88-Day Promise. You feel great about yourself and the results. Now what?

Our lives, like nature, have seasons, patterns, and cycles. And so do energy and the laws of success.

That's why the Post-Promise Plan is an important component to making the 88-Day Promise successful!

What you do after your eighty-eight days can either destroy or support what you did in the 88-Day Promise.

If you were on an eighty-eight-day fitness challenge and then eat everything in sight because you didn't follow a sustainable plan during your 88-Day Promise, it will destroy the gains you made.

If you go on vacation for eighty-eight days after a big 88-Day Promise building your business, you won't have much to come back to.

You cannot totally check out after your 88-Day Promise and reap maximum benefit from your efforts.

What you can do is throttle back. Follow this three-step Post-Promise Plan:

1 Refresh

2 Regroup

3 Recharge

Week One: Refresh

1 **Refresh mentally.** Take a week vacation or place your focus on something entirely different. It is a time to focus on your health and well-being.

2 **Refresh physically.** Eat right. Exercise. Drink lots of water. Get lots of sleep. Get your mind, spirit, and body in a good place.

That's what refreshing looks like. You will still take calls, answer emails, and stay lightly connected, but only if it requires an immediate response.

Week Two: Regroup

1 **Regroup.** Take the week after refreshing to assess your 88-Day Promise.

2 **Document in a journal everything you did.** Document your experiences, thoughts, feelings, and the ups and downs.

3 **Assess what the reinvented you looks like.** What areas do you still want to hone? What adjustments and tweaks do you want to make?

4 **Think back on what you accomplished.** Start planning what the best use of your time and energy is over the next ten weeks to support and tighten up the results you created during the 88-Day Promise.

In business, regrouping means focusing on the team you have built, investing in them, and providing the leadership and training they need.

Weeks Three to Twelve: Recharge

1 Recharge mentally. This is the time for you to grow, read, study, and learn. Read stories of people who have done what you're trying to do. Absorb industry periodicals and training. Take your personal knowledge, skill, and training to the next level.

2 Recharge physically. Rebuild your physical strength. Your body cannot catch up on sleep by sleeping a lot. It takes two or three weeks of getting the right amount of sleep every night after an 88-Day Promise to recalibrate your body.

3 Recharge emotionally. You must prepare yourself mentally and emotionally for the next 88-Day Promise so you have the physical capacity to make it happen.

During your 88-Day Promise, there will be times that you did things for the right reasons, and they seem to bite you later on. You had pure intentions when you started your fitness journey. You started your business for the right reasons and with the right people, strategy, financing, and product/marketing mix.

And when you least expect it, something that was so right during your 88-Day Promise seems to backfire down the road. Expect it—because it will happen. All the results you get during the 88-Day Promise may take months and years to germinate.

But it's still worth it! So much more good comes

from the 88-Day Promise than bad. And even the bad can be good.

You've heard all the expressions about turning lemons into lemonade and that there is a seed of opportunity equal to or greater than the problem. This is no cliché.

When you do the 88-Day Promise with everything you have for a worthy cause you believe in—your health, fitness, family, finances, business, etc.—you cannot lose. You will not regret it even if things don't always seem to be working out how you thought they would.

YOUR 88-DAY
PROMISE

WHAT 88-DAY PROMISE DO you need to start? Do you need to recommit to your physical health? Do you need to recommit to your business? What do you need to give absolutely all of yourself to for eighty-eight days? What do you need to put eighty-eight days of sweat, blood, and tears in? I'm talking enough sweat, blood, and tears to bring tears to the eyes of a Mayflower pilgrim!

What music do you need to record and share?

What talent do you have that you need to share with the world now? What book do you need to write? What mission do you need to conquer? What do you need to fully commit to for the next eighty-eight days?

Decide right now to do it.

Do not wait for Monday. Do not wait for the first of the month. Do not wait for January 1. Start now.

When I decided to get fit, I was at lunch with the senior vice president of Ameriquest Mortgage. My habits changed immediately and were reflected on my afternoon first-class flight back to Florida when I declined the dessert and unhealthy snacks that I had become fond of throughout my travels. Two years later, I was down seventy-five pounds.

When you decide to do the 88-Day Promise, you can't help but start immediately. You just go. You view the time between now and Monday as a head start. You view the time between now and the first of the month as a bonus.

This is about reinventing or changing some aspect

of your life in eighty-eight days. It's transformational. It's empowerment like you've never seen before.

THE 88-DAY PROMISE CAN:

✓ **Transform your life**

✓ **Transform your body**

✓ **Transform your energy**

✓ **Transform your beauty/image/looks**

✓ **Transform your finances**

✓ **Transform your business/career**

✓ **Transform your relationships**

✓ **Transform your thoughts**

THE 88-DAY PROMISE CAN HELP YOU:

✓ **Bounce back from divorce**

✓ **Bounce back from failure**

✓ **Bounce back from self-sabotage**

✓ **Bounce back from weight gain**

✓ **Bounce back from job loss**

So what area of life do you want to change? Not casually wanting to change, but an all-out, 88-Day Promise kind of change?

What do you need to bounce back from, or what aspect do you need to take to the next level?

The 88-Day Promise isn't for those who say they want more; it's for those who are willing to commit to doing whatever it takes—*whatever it takes*—for eighty-eight-plus days. Period.

And when you get to that point, that's when the 88-Day Promise is transformational.

The 88-Day Promise isn't about paying a few dollars and something magical happening. My 88-Day Promise program is demanding. It's not for everyone. Not everybody is ready for an 88-Day Promise. The timing isn't right at every given moment for starting an 88-Day Promise.

It has to be a decision…a decision made with the heart that will be made numerous times throughout the eighty-eight days. And if it lacks conviction out of the gate, it's going to be a long eighty-eight days!

When you're dealing with transformation, people's lives are at stake. Their families, fortunes (or lack thereof), health, self-worth, and reputation are at stake. That's why it's so important that you are in a place that you desperately want change and transformation in an area of your life.

Celebrities, athletes, companies, executives, entre-preneurs, politicians, and leaders from most every walk of life must constantly reinvent themselves to continue their creativity and appeal to their fans and followers. It's a very thin line between just going off the deep end (like we see with some train-wreck celebrity lives) and transformation into something that elevates the playing field and your results. Many of the same variables are in play.

But it's not enough to change your hairstyle, clothes, and where you make appearances; it requires a mental transformation. It's owning who you want to be. It's becoming who you are.

It's time you give yourself permission to be every-thing you were meant to be. Allow yourself to be transformed into your most powerful self. The 88-Day Promise can do that for you.

Everyone should go through an 88-Day Promise, not merely for the results but for the person you become along the way. How your life choices and

preferences change through this awakening and time of transformation will astound you.

You have probably heard the saying "This is an idea whose time has come." Well, I say your time has come. It is time for you to rise up, allow yourself to be transformed, and exercise the boldness and greatness within you. Not for yourself but for the world—for those who will be inspired by your journey and courage, for those who have not said yes to themselves yet. Say yes to who you were meant to be.

Let's do this.

Welcome to the
88-DAY PROMISE!

Dear Friend,

I want to congratulate you on saying yes to your future. The 88-Day Promise has transformed my life in every possible way. Whether your objective is to get fit, grow your business, increase your income, land your dream job, change careers, bounce back from a loss, or run for the senate, the 88-Day Promise is the answer.

The bigger your goal, the more necessary the 88-Day Promise is. Frankly, I love making 88-Day Promises, because they give me something of value to focus on for a specific period of time. I know that giving my all to an area of life that I want to achieve in significantly enhances my quality of life.

Very few people ever do what it takes to win big. You've taken the first step. Over the next twelve weeks, you're going to go from excited, to grinding it out, to fatigue, to just wanting it to be over, to an amazed sense of accomplishment! You'll wonder what's happening to you around eight weeks into it. Expect it. It's normal!

Winners do daily what losers do occasionally. The secret to the 88-Day Promise lies in doing the right things (the critical few) consistently.

Please don't try to take shortcuts on the 88-Day Promise. Earmarking these days for complete focus and devotion is the shortcut!

We are here to support you on your journey. Join the conversation at www.facebook.com/CourageousMedia for support during your 88-Day Promise!

I love you and believe in you!

Dr. RR2

"Goal setting that focuses on outcome instead of process and behavior is why people lose."

—DR. ROLLAN ROBERTS

ACKNOWLEDGMENTS

MY HIGHEST PRAISE GOES to my Lord and Savior, Jesus Christ. Anything I've accomplished has been and will be through His strength and anointing. I must also thank one of my greatest teachers, pain. Pain has taught me more about life and how to think and win than anything else. I've always chosen to feel the pain instead of numbing the pain with vices, and that has served me well. My strongest and most loyal supporters have been my mom and dad, whom I love dearly.

You haven't seen faithful and consistent until you've met my parents. I'm grateful to my spiritual advisers who help me walk daily in integrity, vulnerability, and humility through big wins and dark valleys.

ABOUT THE AUTHOR

Adviser to world governments and nominated to the Civilian Task Force for Central Command and the Department of Defense, Dr. Rollan Roberts is the CEO of Courageous! and America's CEO on iHeart-Radio. He served as CEO of the Hoverboard company, creating the bestselling global consumer product of 2015, and has a record of crafting viral global brands as CEO of both public and private SMB to multibillion-dollar companies. Dr. Roberts provides entrepreneurship programs and events around the world and serves on corporate advisory boards.

Dr. Roberts has addressed world leaders at Harvard University, Bloomberg's BusinessWeek, and China's government and business leaders in Tiananmen Square at the Great Hall of the People (China's Congress). He served as an adviser to the top twenty startup companies in the world (in Spain) and on the U.S.-China Trade War.

In addition to being a private pilot, he hosts Courageous! Entrepreneur Radio, a weekly call-in business program on iHeartRadio, the largest radio and television outlet in America, holds a doctorate degree in global business and entrepreneurship, is the author of four bestselling international books on business and entrepreneurship, was a state senate candidate in 2012, and continues to educate and inspire leaders and entrepreneurs through CEO Huddles and hosting the semi-annual CEO Cruise.

NEW! Only from Simple Truths®

IGNITE READS
spark impact in just one hour

IGNITE READS IS A NEW SERIES OF 1-HOUR READS WRITTEN BY WORLD-RENOWNED EXPERTS!

These captivating books will help you become the best version of yourself, allowing for new opportunities in your personal and professional life. Accelerate your career and expand your knowledge with these powerful books written on today's hottest ideas.

TRENDING BUSINESS AND PERSONAL GROWTH TOPICS

 Read in an hour or less

 Leading experts and authors

 Bold design and captivating content

EXCLUSIVELY AVAILABLE ON SIMPLETRUTHS.COM

Need a training framework?
Engage your team with discussion guides and PowerPoints for training events or meetings.

Want your own branded editions?
Express gratitude, appreciation, and instill positive perceptions to staff or clients by adding your organization's logo to your edition of the book.

Add a supplemental visual experience
to any meeting, training, or event.

Contact us for special corporate discounts!
(800) 900-3427 x247 or simpletruths@sourcebooks.com

LOVED WHAT YOU READ AND WANT MORE?

Sign up today and be the FIRST to receive advance copies of Simple Truths® NEW releases written and signed by expert authors. Enjoy a complete package of supplemental materials that can help you host or lead a successful event. This high-value program will uplift you to be the best version of yourself!

— SIMPLE TRUTHS —
ELITE CLUB
ONE MONTH. ONE BOOK. ONE HOUR.

Your monthly dose of motivation, inspiration, and personal growth.